ABANDONED
WESTERN PENNSYLVANIA

ABANDONED
WESTERN PENNSYLVANIA
SEPARATION FROM A PROUD HERITAGE

CINDY VASKO

After a long absence from photography, music was the catalyst that lured me back to this art form, so thank you, David Cook, for the 2009 concert that redirected my creative path, for, without you, this book would not be. Gratitude is also extended to serendipity for guiding my vision toward a photo of a derelict asylum and prompting an immediate shift in the motion of my photographic endeavors along the abandoned roads less taken. My road trip exploration comrades, however, are the indispensable enhancements of urbex adventures and make these experiences the best times of my life.

America Through Time is an imprint of Fonthill Media LLC
www.through-time.com
office@through-time.com

Published by Arcadia Publishing by arrangement with Fonthill Media LLC
For all general information, please contact Arcadia Publishing:
Telephone: 843-853-2070
Fax: 843-853-0044
E-mail: sales@arcadiapublishing.com
For customer service and orders:
Toll-Free 1-888-313-2665

www.arcadiapublishing.com

First published 2019

Copyright © Cindy Vasko 2019

ISBN 978-1-63499-127-8

All rights reserved. No part of this publication may be reproduced, stored in a retrieval system or transmitted in any form or by any means, electronic, mechanical, photocopying, recording or otherwise, without prior permission in writing from Fonthill Media LLC

Typeset in Trade Gothic 10pt on 15pt
Printed and bound in England

CONTENTS

	Introduction	7
1	Cambria Steel Company	11
2	Carrie Furnaces	16
3	East Broad Top Railroad	27
4	W. A. Young & Sons Foundry and Machine Shop	36
5	Silent Churches	43
6	Roxbury Elementary School	49
7	Ceramics Manufacturer	55
8	The Stillness of Steel Towns	61
9	Overholt Distillery	76
10	Trolley Graveyard	84
11	Waterside Woolen Mill	89
12	Bedford County Jail	96
13	Scotland School for Veterans' Children	101
14	Covered Bridge and Gristmill	111
15	Moose Lodge	119
	About the Author	124
	Bibliography	125

INTRODUCTION

Abandonments are a portent—an omen from our past about our inevitable fate. Abandonments remind us that, ultimately, all will be gone. A forsaken place reveals a crude sense of vulnerability and is simultaneously provocative, intimidating, strange, enthralling, stunning, and alarming. A battle between human will and the relentless forces of nature is pervasive. The marked deterioration of abandonments presents the clash between our human-made formations and nature's power always on its mark and ready to engulf the built environment. Abandonments are cues for the ephemerality of all things. Just like all living things, buildings, and even cities and towns, are mortal.

In my youth, I spent a lot of time exploring the great outdoors, particularly with my father. The woods and parts of the cities I visited often felt like an ethereal realm—extraordinary and novel. I carried this youthful mindset to my current adrenaline-charged explorations of abandonments. Just as I was excited to hunt for unexpected coalfield fossils and crystals during my childhood, today's urban explorations also hold the promise of the unforeseen. One of my motivations with these contemporary adventures is to preserve a photographic account of history before it dissolves. What can we discover about our past and ourselves from these modern remains, especially with an examination of the industrial age vestiges of Western Pennsylvania?

The Rust Belt covers a section of the northeast United States, including a large swathe of Western Pennsylvania where economic decline, population flight, and urban neglect replaced a once-mighty industrial manufacturing sector. The American Dream features a contract for success such that with hard work, one can make a good living and pass it on to their offspring. For so many within the Rust Belt, however, this contract was breached, and perhaps, was only an agreement of blind faith.

The United States is not comfortable with decline. The ostensibly obstinate complications of towns and cities in the Rust Belt regions have often been presented as economic abnormalities, and especially so since Pittsburgh nobly lifted itself from the depths of its decline. The satellite steel towns surrounding Pittsburgh, though, continue to suffer and saw no such Pittsburghian economic recovery. The Western Pennsylvania Rust Belt holds so many embattled steel towns such as Duquesne, Rankin, Homestead, Braddock, McKeesport, Aliquippa, Clairton, Brownsville, and so many more.

Western Pennsylvania Rust Belt towns are declarations to unrelenting farewells: goodbye to a once-robust economy, to a healthy standard of living, to the family home, to neighbors and friends, to a beloved church and school. When the steel industry foundered, many towns dependent upon it died with it. Work vanished and hope died, but the rusting and rotting shells of once-strong Western Pennsylvania manufacturing remain as monuments to better times of the not so distant past.

Pittsburgh, known as the Steel City, rejuvenated its economy. A city that suffered a full breakdown in the early 1980s turned into one of America's best economic revivals by transforming itself with the embrace of trades such as cutting-edge technology, pharmacology, and biology. Not far removed from Pittsburgh, though, are the mill towns unable to escape the obsolescence from the decades since steel production braked in Western Pennsylvania. The steel mills were also the souls of the local businesses and municipal services in Pittsburgh's rim towns, and when the steel soul died, shops and services perished. Pittsburgh's peripheral steel towns are peppered with relics of its past—corroded blast furnace shells, stationary work yard cranes, broken warehouses, still houses of worship, silent schools, plywood main streets, shuttered homes, and empty lots adorned with tall weeds.

I grew up in a town connected to the steel industry: eastern Pennsylvania's Allentown—one of the cities of the industrial triumvirate of the Lehigh Valley; Allentown's neighbor, Bethlehem, was a regional economic driver with its once-formidable Bethlehem Steel. When I drove into Bethlehem at night, Bethlehem Steel's presence was ubiquitous with its steel furnaces illuminating the night sky with a ginger luminosity. This nocturnal industrial ID is no longer a reality, and like my native Lehigh Valley, when I explored Western Pennsylvania, I quickly connected with the attributes of a steel town and recognized the pain of lost dreams.

A good portion of this book reflects a photographic essay about Western Pennsylvania's big steel denouement. Along with Western Pennsylvania steel facilities, so many businesses, services, and even daily life suffered the consequences of being tied to big steel's hip. This book presents Cambria Steel Company, Carrie Furnaces, East Broad Top Railroad, a ceramics factory, Roxbury School, W.A. Young & Sons

Shop Foundry and Machine Shop, houses of worship, and the silent streets of too many rim towns as examples of misplaced faith with big steel's resilience. Other chapters in *Abandoned Western Pennsylvania* reveal forlorn sites not necessarily connected to big steel, although some have indirect ties, as models of lost dreams nevertheless, and include Overholt Distillery, a trolley graveyard, a Moose Lodge, Bedford County Jail, Waterside Woolen Mill, Scotland School for Veterans Children, and a nineteenth-century covered bridge and gristmill.

There is transience in all things, but profound history is ever-present in abandoned buildings and provides evocative revelations of remembrances. When I explore abandonments, I perceive and experience things outside of an ordinary environment with layers of history exposed within the skeletal remains. At a minimum, it is essential to document these forlorn sites and create a relationship with the past for posterity's sake. Look through my eyes, and see the architectural hereafter, historical conservancy, and a photographic memoir of Western Pennsylvania.

1

CAMBRIA STEEL COMPANY

Johnstown, Pennsylvania, is famous for three devastating floods, and especially the tragic flood of 1889 that claimed over 2,000 lives. Before this historical Johnstown marker, however, an essential iron and steel mill established a large footprint on Johnstown's landscape and sealed its eminent muscle in the Western Pennsylvania region.

The 1840s witnessed the arrival of iron and steel in Johnstown, spurred in part by the launch of the Pennsylvania Railroad. By 1852, the flourishing iron and steel industry brought forth Cambria Iron Company, later renamed Cambria Steel Company ("Cambria") in 1898, with Bethlehem Steel purchasing Cambria from Midvale Steel and Ordnance Company in 1923. Cambria was one of the largest producers of rail track in the United States, and also served as the model for the large wave of steel mills, such as Bethlehem Steel Company and the U.S. Steel Corporation, making debuts in the late nineteenth and early twentieth centuries.

As Cambria expanded, many southern and eastern European immigrants claimed Johnstown as their home and Cambria as their work home. During the 1970s, Cambria abridged its operations because its facilities were aging, environmental compliance became problematic, but, most importantly, overseas suppliers invaded Cambria's slice of the trade pie, resulting in several Cambria reductions in force during the 1970s and 1980s.

Because the Cambria complex held the most intact structures dating from America's earliest steel operations, the National Park Service honored Cambria with a National Historic Landmark designation in 1989. This badge of honor, though, was unable to save Cambria from its ultimate fate. The final 1,200 Cambria workers received pink slips in 1992 when Cambria shuttered its operations.

Cambria's historically significant and oldest building is the Blacksmith Shop.

The Blacksmith Shop fashioned an assortment of items with the iron and steel, manufactured in the adjacent Cambria shops. Walking into the Blacksmith Shop is like being inside of a time capsule, as it still retains the nineteenth- and early twentieth-century tools and machinery.

Today, Cambria is undergoing a minor economic recovery with light industrial manufacturers assuming part of the complex. Additionally, a medical marijuana company recently received approval for the establishment of plant-growing operations within a large portion of the mill. Marijuana in a steel mill? I wonder what the early Cambria ironworkers would think of their mill's repurpose. A new business is indeed growing in Johnstown.

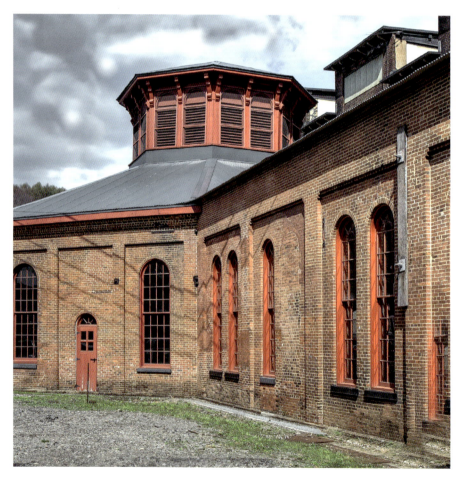

BLACKSMITH SHOP: Cambria Steel Company's Blacksmith Shop was responsible for producing a variety of products from the iron and steel manufactured in an adjacent Cambria mill.

OLDEST BLACKSMITH SHOP SECTION: The Blacksmith shop has three sections. The oldest portion was completed in 1864 and has an octagonal ceiling and cupola, and contains heavy-timbered roof trusses. The remaining two shop sections were completed in the 1870s and 1880s.

10-TON STEAM-POWERED HAMMER: The Smithsonian Institution owns the steam-powered hammer, but it is housed in the Blacksmith Shop.

BLACKSMITH SHOP MACHINERY: The Blacksmith Shop offers students an opportunity to learn the traditional methods of blacksmithing.

CAMBRIA BUILDING GRAFFITI REFLECTING LAYOFFS OF THE 1980s: The graffiti etched on the exterior of a Cambria Steel Company building reflects the community's pain of steel industry layoffs.

THE SILENT CAMBRIA STEEL WORK YARD: Shortly after Cambria closed its doors in 1992, Johnstown was designated as a distressed community under Pennsylvania's Municipalities Recovery Act of 1993.

2

CARRIE FURNACES

During its lifecycle, the Homestead Works of U.S. Steel Corporation and its open-hearth mills produced nearly one-third of all steel used in the United States. This facility along the riverbanks of the Monongahela in Homestead, a few miles outside of Pittsburgh, covered 450 acres and employed more than 200,000 throughout its operations. The adjacent Carrie Furnace site, built in 1881, absorbed by U.S. Steel Corporation in 1901, produced iron for the Homestead Works until its closure in 1978.

Numbers six and seven Carrie furnaces are the last-standing blast furnaces. The blast furnaces are monuments to pre-World War II iron-making technology and stand tall as an homage to the industry that drove the local economy and impacted national economic policy. A total of 3,000 workers once toiled at the Carrie site. The Rivers of Steel Corporation allows tours of the Carrie property for a proper tribute to these relics.

As a photographer, on three occasions, I was fortunate to join a group at the Carrie site and have somewhat free reign to capture Carrie's rusted beauty. In addition to Carrie's two furnaces, one finds an oversized brick blower house, an ore yard, a car dumper, a torpedo car, the blowing engine house, hot stoves, the cast house and a 15-ton gantry crane that moved iron ore.

The redevelopment efforts of Allegheny County, several municipalities, and the Steel Industry Heritage Council aim to refurbish Carrie into an interactive museum, but environmental cleanup of the site must be completed before the implementation of any plans. The area surrounding Carrie is part of a long-term mixed-use development plan of housing, hotels, and a conference center. Carrie's proud heritage is embedded in the steel found in the Empire State Building, Battleship Missouri, Gateway Arch, Sears Tower, The Golden Gate Bridge, Panama Canal, United Nations Building, the George Washington Bridge, and Alaska oil pipeline.

BLAST FURNACE: At its peak production period, the Carrie Furnaces produced 1,000–1,250 tons of iron each day. In the early 1900s, the Carrie Furnaces were part of a chain of forty-eight blast furnaces in the Pittsburgh metropolitan area. The two remaining Carrie Blast Furnaces are thirteen stories tall and are National Historic Landmarks.

CONVEYOR: Coal is dumped into large ovens and heated to 2,400 degrees Fahrenheit for coal's gas removal and conversion to coke. The coke, along with iron ore and limestone, travels on the conveyor to the top of the blast furnace for heating and liquefying.

▶ **BLAST FURNACE MOLTEN METAL CHANNEL:** Molten metal at 2,700 degrees would flow through the channel of the furnace after hot gusts of air melt it in the blast furnace. The blast furnace walls are made of 2½-inch-thick steel plate and include a layer of refractory brick.

▼ **BLAST FURNACE:** A 4-ton liquefied combination of iron ore, coke, and limestone produced 1 ton of iron. Molten iron cooling required a daily allotment of up to 5 million gallons of water.

BOILER SHOP: The boiler shop fabricated plate work and manufactured pressure and non-pressure tanks.

TORPEDO LADLE CAR: Torpedo ladle cars transferred molten iron from the iron making section of Carrie, across the hot metal bridge over the Monongahela River to the U.S. Steel Homestead Works.

GANTRY CRANE: A gantry crane moves on a horizontal plane and straddles an object or workspace. The entire structure, including the gantry, allows for movement along rails.

TRESTLE SPAN WITH VIEW OF HOT STOVES, GANTRY CRANE AND CONVEYOR: Blast furnaces were named after women. Carrie was a family name of one of the early owners.

MAZE OF PIPING AND RUSTY VATS: Because the soil was contaminated with PCBs and sulfates, environmental assessments of the site ensued. The first site mitigation phase completed in 2007 and the second phase is underway.

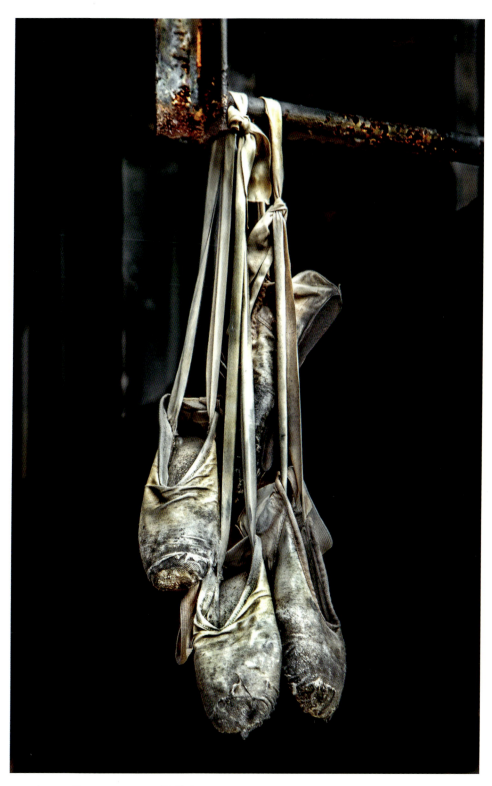

REMAINS: Years ago, a group of ballerinas visited Carrie Furnace and left their pointe shoes—perhaps this is their unique, soft form of tagging.

TUNNEL: The bins on the side of the tunnel stored raw materials for iron production, such as limestone, iron ore, and coke.

ABANDONED TRAIN CAR: Although much of the graffiti found on the Carrie site is unwanted, the Rivers of Steel operators cooperate with the art community and allow artists to paint their "art" on designated walls. By doing this, the amount of unwanted tagging has lessened.

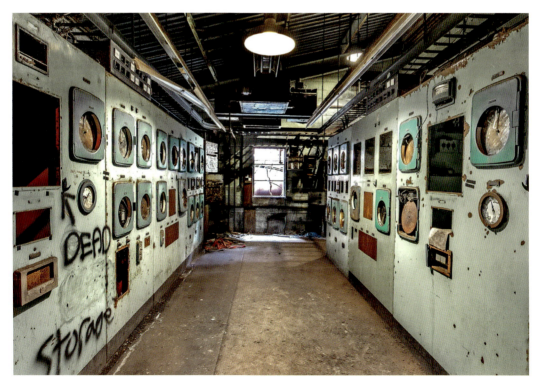

CONTROL ROOM: While Carrie's peak production occurred in the 1950s and 1960s, Pittsburgh, however, known as the Steel City, reached its peak in 1910 with Pittsburgh producing more than 60 percent of the total United States steel production.

CARRIE DEER: The Carrie Deer, also called the Rankin Deer, stands between the blower facility and blast furnace. This art installation is 45 feet tall and 35 feet wide and made of pipes and other recycled materials found on the site. Six artists from the Industrial Arts Collective created the deer in 1997–1998.

3

EAST BROAD TOP RAILROAD

We do not ride upon the railroad; it rides upon us.

Henry David Thoreau

The railroad was both a symbol of the Industrial Revolution and a profound nineteenth-century societal dynamic. In the United States, the railroad was celebrated as a vehicle supporting the doctrine of Manifest Destiny by way of the Transcontinental Railroad's cross-country connection. In a nation lacking accessible roads before the birth of the railroad, the railroad allowed commercial markets to flourish on a national scale, as well as smaller, but no less important local sectors, such as the community of Rockhill.

Rockhill's East Broad Top Railroad and Coal Company ("EBT") was chartered in 1856 and supported the quarrying and transportation of coal from the coal mines along nearby Broad Top Mountain. In 1873, the first section of 3-foot narrow-gauge track was completed with a route from Mount Union to Rockhill Furnace. The following year, the line extended to Robertsdale, and in 1892, the line stretched to Woodvale. The northern terminus at Mount Union connected with the standard gauge Pennsylvania Railroad. Eventually, EBT established passenger service for its train routes. Rockville was the hub for EBT engine shops and terminals. The EBT compound was a complete operation of service facilities.

EBT was a profitable transporter of coal, but eventually, rising labor costs, fading coal deposits, and labor strikes negatively impacted EBT. Additionally, when steel became the favored metal at the expense of iron, the Rockhill Iron Furnace closed and EBT suffered a loss of traffic. Finally, many local factories switched their fuel sources from coal to oil and gas, thus prompting another monetary shock to EBT.

With the lack of coal sales and the preference of steel over iron, EBT was forced to close its operation on April 15, 1956. Just as Henry David Thoreau's words are prophetic to many casualties of the industrial revolution, EBT was not an exception as technology is often an improved means to an unimproved end.

EBT earned a National Historic Landmark status in 1963. In 1983, The Friends of East Broad Top, Inc. formed with a goal of EBT preservation and restoration. Even though EBT was not directly joined with Western Pennsylvania's big steel economy, the influence of big steel impacted the economic health of the EBT, and eventually, EBT united with the growing mound of industrial casualties.

EAST BROAD TOP RAILROAD ("EBT") COMPOUND: Although EBT dates to the pre-Civil War period, with the commencement of the Civil War, railroad construction funding was delayed and the EBT between Mt. Union and Rockhill Furnace was not completed until 1873.

STEAM LOCOMOTIVE IN EBT ROUNDHOUSE: EBTs roundhouse, built in 1882, is one of the oldest railroad roundhouses in the United States. The roundhouse holds six steam locomotives dating to 1911.

ROUNDHOUSE LEFTOVERS: The roundhouse contains a 1927 gas-electric railcar that was used to transport mail and passengers along the railroad's 33 miles of track.

▼ **EAST BROAD TOP RAILROAD RAIL YARD:** EBT hauled coal, lumber, ganister rock, concrete, road tar, pig iron, agricultural commodities, general freight, and passengers. During the first thirty years, EBT supplied much of its coal to the Rockhill Iron Furnace and, in turn, transported pig iron from the furnace operations.

▶ **MACHINE SHOP:** During the early 1900s, EBT introduced new steam engines and railcars. The machine shop was renovated and much of what is seen at the machine shop today is because of this modernization.

◄ **1920 BALDWIN LOCOMOTIVE:** EBT transported semi-bituminous coal from the mines on the east side of the Broad Top Mountain to the Pennsylvania Railroad in Mount Union.

▼ **M4 SWITCHER TRAIN:** Rockhill's 1960 bicentennial featured an EBT excursion along the railroad's old route. The EBT tours occurred every year until December 2011.

COAL BUNKERS AND ABANDONED HOPPER CARS IN DISTANCE: The coal from the Broad Top Mountain region was known for its clean burning properties and was the preference for the fire-brick plants in Mount Union, as well as the World War II ships.

BLACKSMITH SHOP: EBT is unique in that it is an all-inclusive preserved original railroad instead of a collection of components from various railroad locations.

▲ **OPEN AIR OBSERVATION AND HOPPER CARS:** An unusual attribute about EBT is its narrow-gauge line. Instead of using the standard rail width of 4 feet 8½ inches, EBT rails are separated by 3 feet.

◄ **BLACKSMITH SHOP:** EBT was profitable from the 1880s through the 1940s, and some of these profits modernized EBT infrastructure.

MACHINE SHOP: When the region's iron industry waned in the early 1900s, the railroad depended on coal traffic for about 90 percent of its revenue.

4

W. A. YOUNG & SONS FOUNDRY AND MACHINE SHOP

Walking through the door of W. A. Young & Sons Foundry and Machine Shop ("W. A. Young") in Rices Landing is akin to stepping into another era. The preservation of W. A. Young's contents is astonishing, as everything was left just as it was when the foundry and machine shop closed its doors in 1965. The W. A. Young facility is a pristine example of early twentieth-century industrial heritage. The two-story building on the banks of the Monongahela River is owned and managed by the Rivers of Steel National Heritage Area group, and embraces the objective of preserving this site's historical value.

W. A. Young built the machine shop in 1900 with lumber from the family farm. A foundry joined the shop in 1908 and electricity made its appearance in 1928. The shop initially repaired boats and later served regional and local clients' needs for the creation of goods such as bronze castings, pipe fittings, and locomotive wheels among other things. The shop also contributed to the two world war efforts.

All of the equipment in the shop dates from 1870 to 1920. A complex array of belts and pulleys throughout the shop operates twenty-five machines, and each is independent of the other and fully operational by one motor.

W. A. Young shuttered its doors in 1965 and left behind all of its contents for posterity. Several factors led to W. A. Young's closing: the decline in coal production with consequential forced reductions in work orders from coal companies; the U.S. Army Corps of Engineers demolition of the navigation lock at Rices Landing, and the resultant curtailment of dynamic river commerce within the local community; the Interstate Highway System negatively impacting the fruitfulness of local business with the diversion of traffic from this area; and W. A. Young clients purchasing nationally distributed merchandise as a result of improved transportation.

EXTERIOR OF W. A. YOUNG & SONS FOUNDRY AND MACHINE SHOP: This family-owned, turn of the twentieth-century foundry and machine shop performed custom orders for a variety of clients.

FOUNDRY SECTION CASTING TUMBLER: Cast items were added to the tumbler's drum and tumbled until the rough edges were smoothed and finished.

BLACKSMITH SECTION: Eventually, the W. A. Young & Sons foundry faced competition from more extensive and more efficient foundries in the Pittsburgh metropolitan region. Ultimately, W. A. Young & Sons was no longer cost-effective with its production of castings, and thus forced to function exclusively as a machine shop.

MACHINE SHOP: Throughout its operations, W. A. Young & Sons only employed a few foundry workers for the operation of the cupola furnace and casting process.

EMPTY WHISKEY BOTTLES: After the founder, William Young, passed away, Young's sons, Walter and Carl, operated the business and kept the payroll under five, because they wanted to avoid union establishment at the shop.

MACHINE SHOP: During World War II, W. A. Young & Sons participated in war training programs and offered training with metal crafts and machine tool operations, such as lathes, shapers, drill presses, planers, and grinders.

FOUNDRY SECTION LARGE LADLE: Molten metal was tapped from the furnace and into a ladle, and then the molten metal poured into molds. The foundry's floor is dirt to minimize of fire hazards.

◄ **FOUNDRY SECTION:** A belt-driven line shaft system powered W. A. Young & Sons machines. The main belt turned the shaft and also powered a connecting line shaft in the Pattern Shop.

▼ **DISCARDED WORK CLOTHES AND SHOES IN FOUNDRY SECTION:** Because of its complete collection of machinery and tools, W. A. Young & Sons earned the status as a National Historic Landmark in 2017.

5

SILENT CHURCHES

Frequently, when people settle in an area, one of the first things they do as a group is to organize a center of worship because their faith is a focal point of their lives. Western Pennsylvania religious congregations are adjusting to a new reality as they cope with so many church closures and mergers and the loss of their spiritual homes. So many of these houses of faith were built with majesty and old-world craftsmanship and allowed several generations to participate in baptisms, weddings, and funerals. The author does not identify this church and instead wants to present it as a parallel example to so many steel town area churches in Western Pennsylvania.

Many churches in Western Pennsylvania were constructed at a time serving the influx of new immigrants in the late nineteenth century and early twentieth century. The population in Western Pennsylvania spiked as waves of immigrants arrived to work in the local industrial factories. In the manufacturing region of Western Pennsylvania, the settlements of the various ethnic groups constructed houses of worship catering to their cultural roots, such as the ethnicities of Hungary, Slovakia, Croatia, Poland, and Germany. Church attendance peaked in the 1940s and 1950s, but many Western Pennsylvania churches suffered shaky realities beginning in the 1960s.

These once-thriving steel town churches struggled with the impact of an aging population, as well as the severe economic changes to their community post-World War II. Many of these parishioners employed by the area's steel mills saw not only their source of employment wither away but also the shuttering of their beloved churches. On many levels, a church closure, like the steel industry, reflects the failure to adapt to shifting circumstances. The church closure also represents the passing of a community whose members devoted so much of their time, drive and affection to their church only to realize the result of sorrow and defeat. When a beloved church closes, the loss is wistful to many: it rips a hole in the heart of the neighborhood as it seizes safety and comfort from those knotted with their sacred homes.

CATHOLIC CHURCH NAVE: The church was established in 1899. The painted cityscape behind the altar is likely from the hand of a post-church closure graffitist.

PEWS: Some of the pews are inscribed with parishioners' names.

BALCONY: By the 1990s, the population numbers in this steel town plunged so much that the diocese could no longer support many of the parishes.

NAVE: The Gothic-style church still holds the beauty of its rosettes, arches, and chandeliers.

MUSIC BOOK: When the church shuttered in 2002, the book was closed on five generations of families that attended baptisms, marriages, and funerals at this church.

DISCARDED OFFERTORY ENVELOPES: During the church's peak attendance years just after World War II, about 300 families were congregation members.

◀ **STAINED-GLASS NAVE WINDOW:** After World War II, the town population dwindled and the numbers attending church services in this area declined as the younger families preferred churches based on proximity to their homes rather than for tradition or ethnic heritage.

▼ **FORLORN MISSAL:** During the church's 103 years of worship, it had only four pastors.

6

ROXBURY ELEMENTARY SCHOOL

A closed school is a painful loss to a community with its once busy classrooms and corridors, now lifeless and forlorn. Neighborhoods feel more ownership over a shuttered school compound than perhaps over other abandoned buildings. Schools serve many roles for assorted patrons. Schools, of course, educate students, but they also steer employment of teachers and staff. Schools are places where societal linkages cultivate, and where caring connections develop and endure among families, teachers, and community. Additionally, schools are aligned with local organizations and the networks of churches, nonprofit organizations, and social service groups, upon which all can be vital components toward the assistance and care of pupils. A school is not just an assembly: it embodies a community, a social link, and the focus of town life. The closing of the Roxbury School in Johnstown must seem like the loss of a community friend. Unfortunately, school closures are not exclusive to Western Pennsylvania and are becoming a nationwide trend.

The baby boom after World War II forced a school building expansion, but as the children of this era grew up and moved from their hometowns, and also had fewer children, school enrollments dropped. Additionally, deep educational budget cuts, and the loss of income drivers in many urban centers, such as Cambria Steel Company in Johnstown, and the steel factories in neighboring Pittsburgh communities, accelerated the trend of school closures within the Western Pennsylvania region.

Vacant for over twenty years, Roxbury School was built in 1908. Roxbury was demolished in late 2017 to make way for a senior living apartment complex.

ROXBURY SCHOOL: Roxbury Elementary School was built in 1901 and closed in 1997.

CLASSROOM: Roxbury expanded its footprint in 1913.

▲ **OFFICE:** Manufacturing in the Western Pennsylvania region collapsed, and it affected all community sectors, including the viability of schools. Lacking resources, the unemployed left the area in a mass exodus.

▶ **MOSSY CLASSROOM FLOOR:** The Roxbury neighborhood is part of Johnstown with a population of 20,000. The city of Johnstown lost population for nine decades, falling by 70 percent from its peak in 1920.

CLASSROOM: A significant challenge for many Rust Belt communities, large and small, centers on the economic transformation of low-skill factory jobs and paternal company town employers to more diverse and dynamic entrepreneurial economies.

STAIRCASE: There are more than 1,000 vacant buildings in Johnstown, including homes, and it would cost about 10 million to tear down all of the abandonments, but the city only has enough money to tear down about thirty buildings each year.

FACULTY LOUNGE: Like Roxbury, declining enrollments and prolonged budget stress are prompting schools across the country to close.

LUNCHROOM: Roxbury School was afflicted with lead and asbestos and had to undergo abatement procedures before its demolition.

ROXBURY SCHOOL: The Roxbury Elementary School bell was saved when the school was demolished in late 2017 to make way for senior housing.

7

CERAMICS MANUFACTURER

Like a black hole, the crumpled steel belt sucked the life out of so many local businesses, and this Western Pennsylvania ceramics company could not escape the tug of regional economic distress. Even though this ceramics company ceased operations in 1991, it holds a rich history dating back to 1901. As one walks through the vast deserted space of this once proud manufacturer, one can imagine the satisfaction of the workers making products that were not only beautiful but also practical. The company's ceramics products appealed to all and appeared on the tables of diplomats as well as the local steelworker.

At its height of production in the post-World War II period, the ceramics company employed more than 3,000. By 1948, the company occupied 16 acres with 700,000 square feet of manufacturing space and managed the production of 145,000 pieces of ceramics each day.

The ceramics company was the first of its kind in this region but was not the first to fail in the Rust Belt area. The ceramics company implemented valiant efforts to stay afloat with improvements to machinery and products, along with rollouts of robust advertising programs. These actions, however, were not enough to stave off the imminent collapse of this local company. The ceramics company surrendered to the specters of the region's big steel collapse, including collapsed steel's side effects of high regional unemployment and population flight. Adding to the black hole business stew is overseas competition with a large grab of the ceramics trade, increased labor costs and disputes making too many appearances, and a change in the ceramics company corporate leadership that cultivated internal instability with resistance to appeasement.

This manufacturing facility was more than just a paycheck to the people that worked here. This loss, just like the loss of steel manufacturing, is a significant event that rippled through families and communities and unraveled the region's social fabric.

CERAMICS STORAGE AREA: The Company initially manufactured queensware dinnerware (cream-colored earthenware) for hotels and institutions and later diversified its product base with the addition of several lines of fine china.

ENDLESS DISCARDED CERAMICS: In 1936, Theodore Haviland of France's Limoges China feared a second war was brewing in Europe and searched for a safe environment to manufacture Limoges China. He selected the Pennsylvania Company to produce the high-quality Limoges China.

WAREHOUSE: At the commencement of World War II, the Company deferred fine china production and instead manufactured china for the army and navy and also produced porcelain components for landmines. In 1945, the manufacture of fine china resumed.

PRODUCTION AREA: By 1927, the company was the country's leading manufacturer of hotel and restaurant ceramics.

▲ **FACTORY EXTERIOR:** After World War II, United States economic prosperity contributed to the success of the ceramics factory.

◄ **DECAL STORAGE:** Decals were applied to ceramics and also provided customization of logos and designs. After application of the decal, water bubbles beneath the decal were removed to ensure complete contact with the ceramics pieces.

▶ **VIEW FROM SECOND FLOOR:** The company's clients were vast—American Legions, Pennsylvania and Baltimore & Ohio railroads, World War I hospitals in France, the Century of Progress exhibit at the 1933 Chicago World's Fair, 1939 New York World's Fair, the White House, the Waldorf Astoria Hotel, Republican National Committee, Ethiopian Emperor Haile Selassie, and the Strategic Air Command.

▼ **CRATES AWAITING SHIPMENT THAT WILL NEVER OCCUR:** The Company introduced a tunnel kiln—an innovation in ceramics production, which created stronger ceramics in less time.

◀ **MOSSY WAREHOUSE:** Like Theodore Haviland of Limoges, Louis E. Hellman of the Rosenthal China Company in Germany sought a market for the production of his fine china for the American market at the dawn of World War II and reached a production agreement with the Pennsylvania ceramics company.

▼ **LEFTOVERS:** Since the 1950s, the influx of imported ceramics created a sustained economic problem for the company, with the situation escalating in the 1980s.

8

THE STILLNESS OF STEEL TOWNS

Town by town, factory by factory, job by job. A tide of change.

Pittsburgh Press
December 5, 1982

Big steel created a societal foundation—a muscular industrial dynamo for Pittsburgh's regional economy, as well as the nation. At World War II's end, no industrial sector was more vital to America's economic health than American steel. Over the last six decades, however, big steel faced a persistent waning, becoming less competitive and less fundamental to the United States economy. So much was lost: jobs, people, and vitality.

The reasons for the downfall of big steel are many: lack of innovation, foreign competition, labor strikes, the 1970s OPEC oil embargo, and a transition to a United States service economy among other reasons. All of these reasons are little comfort for the citizens that served the big steel corporations in Western Pennsylvania, especially for Pittsburgh's satellite towns, where economic decline, population loss, and urban deterioration replaced the economic boom that was once characteristic of this region. Some of these towns border on ghost town status, with empty sidewalks and endless shuttered storefronts. One Pittsburgh satellite town lost 90 percent of its population since the apex of steel production.

So much is lost in an area where steel continues to imprint on Western Pennsylvania identities. Even though the city of Pittsburgh has recovered from steel's plunge, the satellite towns have not mended and continue to suffer; yet many within this metropolitan circle remain entrenched in steel roots, and steel loyalty runs deep. How can big steel not be a source of pride when steel's signature is stamped on so many national brands, such as the Empire State Building, United Nations Building, US Steel Building, Chrysler Building, Houston Astrodome, Louisiana Superdome, Gateway Arch in St. Louis, Brooklyn Bridge, George Washington Bridge, Mackinac Straits span in Michigan, San Francisco–Oakland Bay Bridge, Sears (now Willis) Tower, Transcontinental Railroad and subsequent railroads, Rockefeller Center, the war materiel for World War II, and, last but not least, the cherished Pittsburgh Steelers football franchise?

Memories of a noble past are difficult to sever, and psychologists note that clinging to positive recollections helps one deal with difficult circumstances. Many of those within the Western Pennsylvania steel town clutch the memories of a time when steel was king but also latch on to the eternal hope of an economic rejuvenation akin to that of their big brother, Pittsburgh.

BARBER SHOP: A barber shop is closed in a once-thriving steel town. In the 1940s, more than half of the world's steel was produced by American steel mills and about 40 percent in the 1950s.

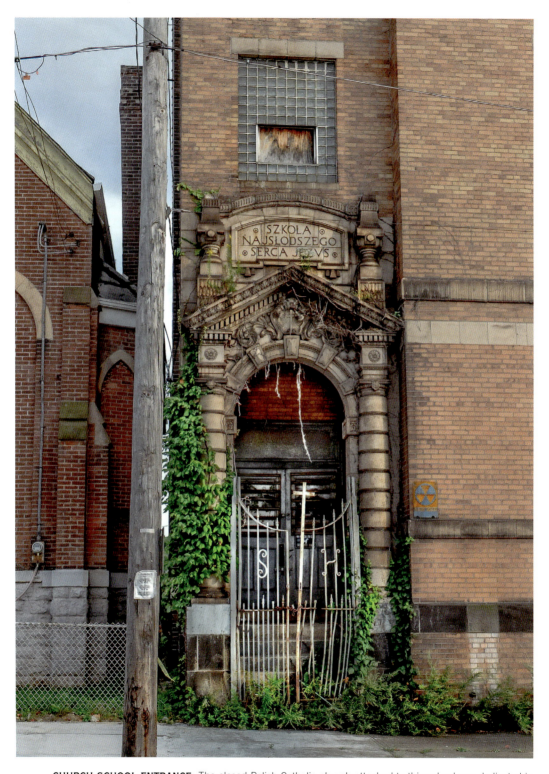

CHURCH SCHOOL ENTRANCE: The closed Polish Catholic church attached to this school was dedicated in 1897, and its parishioner rolls expanded rapidly following World War I. After World War II, the population of the town decreased from 22,000 to its present 8,500. The parish closed in 1970.

LOCAL HOTEL: All businesses in steel towns suffered after the 1970s. In 1948, there were about 700,000 steelworkers, and today 83,000 work in the nation's steel mills.

CHURCH: Just as businesses closed when manufacturing took a nosedive, local churches suffered too. This row house church in a neighborhood adjacent to a steel mill lost its footing when big steel collapsed.

CHURCH INTERIOR: Although this town still has an operating steel mill, albeit, at a significantly reduced capacity, the flight of the town's population forced this church to close its doors.

MAIN ARTERY THROUGH THE CENTER OF TOWN: A town that once prospered as a steamboat builder, and later as a railroad yard and robust coking center, is nearly empty of residents and activity.

FORMER HOTEL AND APARTMENT COMPLEX: When the manufacturing industries that supported the steel sector left this town, so did the people, and the community now resembles a ghost town.

ELEVATOR AND STAIRCASE OF FORMER HOTEL AND APARTMENT COMPLEX: At one time, the population of this town was 8,000, and now it is only about 2,500.

▲ **APARTMENT:** The manufacturing dip began in the 1970s, and by the dawn of the 1980s, a mass exodus of population from steel town satellites commenced.

▶ **APARTMENT:** In the 1980s, work disappeared, businesses shuttered, and a working wage to support a family could no longer be had for too many residents.

◄ **APARTMENT:** Although a few mom and pop businesses still reside in some of the buildings on the town's main street, most of the shops are boarded and crumbling, such as this apartment complex.

▼ **BANK VAULT:** Banks of the past were often ornate and large, and this abandoned bank was not the exception. This bank closed after the steel community suffered and the town's population left.

BANK LOBBY: Large and ornamental is no longer a must for bank architecture. Electronic bank transactions and deregulation contributed to the demise of elegant bank design.

SWEET SHOP WITH SODA FOUNTAIN COUNTER: A glimpse of past simpler times where a long counter was lined with chrome stools and bright metal mechanisms that once operated under the skilled hand of a soda jerk.

SODA FOUNTAIN AND ICE CREAM TOPPING CANISTERS: The soda fountain made its debut at the dawn of the twentieth century and continued until it withered away in the 1970s, and at the time when big steel buckled.

APARTMENT BUILDING: The Western Pennsylvania regional role during World War II was the "Arsenal of Democracy." Big steel manufactured 95 million tons of steel, 52 million artillery shells, 11 million explosives, and earned a worldwide reputation for industrial strength.

CHURCH: A church endures not merely for its congregation but the greater good of the community. A church is a shelter for those in need of an escape from the stresses of life.

▲ **HOSPITAL:** A closed hospital is a significant loss to a community and especially for this town that was built by railroaders and coal miners.

◀ **CHURCH ENTRANCE:** All church denominations share the same plight as the economic vise continues to tighten within the region. The Pittsburgh Catholic diocese recently announced a second round of church closures and will reduce the current 188 parishes over six counties to fifty-seven starting in 2020.

9

OVERHOLT DISTILLERY

Too much of anything is bad, but too much good whiskey is barely enough.

Mark Twain

For more than 200 years, Old Overholt whiskey was treasured, identified as medicine during Prohibition, and featured in an HBO miniseries, *Boardwalk Empire*. Founded in 1810, Overholt was the first commercial distillery in the United States. Rye whiskey, aged in oak barrels for four years, was Overholt Distillery's recipe for success and the old derelict distillery in Broad Ford has an illustrious past.

Abraham Overholt transformed the craft of distilling rye whiskey on the family farm into a viable business. Abraham and his brother, Christian, constructed a log cabin distillery in southwestern Pennsylvania and produced rye whiskey. A few years later, a larger stone distillery was built and increased capacity ten-fold. Demand for Overholt whiskey was so high that, in 1855, the family set up a second distillery at Broad Ford because of its river access. The distillery expanded in 1867 with a higher whiskey output. When Abraham Overholt died in 1870, his grandson, industrialist Henry Clay Frick, assumed ownership. During the mid-1870s, the distillery branded the whiskey as Old Overholt and featured Abraham's likeness on the label.

During the onset of Prohibition, the southwestern Pennsylvania distillery closed and never reopened. Secretary of Treasury Andrew Mellon, however, granted himself a medicinal whiskey license and allowed the Broad Ford distillery to sell prescription whiskey. When Prohibition ended, whiskey production resumed at the distillery. Old Overholt quickly became the bestselling rye whiskey in the United States.

Over the years, though, consumer tastes altered with a preference for bourbon whiskey over rye as well as an eventual shift in liquor preferences away from whiskey in general. Currently, however, cocktails and especially whiskey are once again in the spotlight, with Old Overholt returning to favor within some of the new hip taste circles.

The Broad Ford plant closed in 1950 and moved production of Old Overholt to a nearby distillery in West Elizabeth. Between 1960 and 1970, Old Overholt production moved to Kentucky and is now under the crafting hand of Jim Beam Distillers.

The Broad Ford distillery has been shuttered for almost seventy years and has been the victim of several fires and vandalism. Overholt has a peculiar tie to big steel even though Overholt's demise in Broad Ford is not the result of the steel collapse. Henry Clay Frick swelled the family's fortune and dynasty with steel industry coke ovens, courtesy of the profits from Overholt. Just like the industrial shells in steel towns, Overholt's ruins still stand like proud pillars to a storied time in American history.

OVERHOLT GRAIN ELEVATOR, GRANARY AND SMOKE STACK IN FOREGROUND, WITH DISTILLERY IN BACKGROUND: At one time, the granary held a steel conveyor that connected to the distillery, which moved grain from the storehouse to the distillery.

GRAIN FUNNEL BENEATH GRAIN SILO: The 1910 100th anniversary of Overholt rye whiskey was a prosperous time for the company. At this time, Overholt was one of the largest and most valued whiskey-makers in the country.

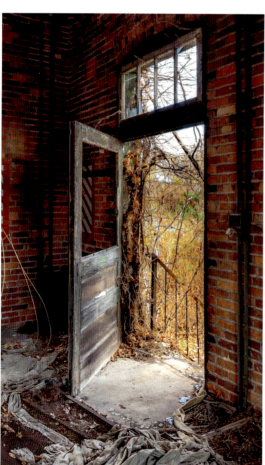

WAREHOUSE SIDE ENTRANCE: The warehouse is a two-story brick building with a tin roof.

DISTILLERY: During Prohibition, the distillery in southwestern Pennsylvania shut down, but the Broad Ford facility distilled medicinal whiskey.

WAREHOUSE: Old Overholt whiskey is named for Abraham Overholt, the grandfather of the wealthy American Industrialist, Henry Clay Frick.

DISTILLERY: When Abraham Overholt died in 1870, ownership eventually transferred into the hands of his grandson, Henry Clay Frick, best known for his business with purified coal, or coke.

OFFICE BUILDING: The HBO series *Boardwalk Empire* features Overholt Distillery.

DISTILLERY VAT: The peak of the rye whiskey business was during the 1880s. Ulysses S. Grant drank Old Overholt, as did John Henry "Doc" Holliday and John F. Kennedy.

OFFICE: In 1854, the large distillery at Broad Ford sat on the banks of the Youghiogheny River and next to the railroad tracks of the new Pittsburgh and Connellsville Railroad. The business incorporated as A. Overholt & Co. in 1858.

DISTILLERY: Even though Overholt's 200th anniversary in 2010 was subdued, for more than 150 years, Overholt was the gold standard for quality whiskey.

10

TROLLEY GRAVEYARD

They told me to take a streetcar named Desire, and then transfer to one called Cemeteries and ride six blocks and get off at—Elysian Fields!

A Streetcar Named Desire

Just as one watched Blanche—the protagonist in Tennessee Williams's play *A Streetcar Named Desire*—face the path of her symbolic death as she arrives at Elysian Fields (Greek mythology's land of the dead), one senses the passing of something extraordinary as well as another type of figurative defeat upon seeing the endless array of discarded trolley cars in a wooded graveyard. This vehicle graveyard represents the loss of simplicity and charm when streetcars were the preferred mode of urban transportation.

Removed from sight and secluded in the woods, one suddenly sees seemingly endless rows of World War II-era trolleys, also known as streetcars. The colorful vehicle spectacle embraces over fifty-six abandoned trolleys from Boston, Cincinnati, Chicago, Kansas City, Cleveland, Pittsburgh, and Philadelphia. Some Philadelphia Septa commuter cars join the trolley's neighborhood too. This transportation depository is a dystopian sight with trees and leaves competing with steel carcasses for space and in several instances, claiming a footing inside of the trolley cars.

The trolleys are part of a private collection. The owner purchased many of them in the 1980s when idle fleets were auctioned by rail services. The trolleys were put on flatbeds and transported to their Western Pennsylvania wooded home. Some trolley cars have been restored, and others are undergoing restoration as the diverse lot of cars rest in their distinct Elysian Fields.

YELLOW PITTSBURGH AREA TRANSIT TROLLEY, AND LINE OF GREEN BOSTON MBTA CARS: The "T" logo was first used on MBTA trolleys in 1964 and well after their manufacture. The MBTA in Boston still uses some of the same types of cars, but facing problems with a dearth of spare parts.

PCC PENNSYLVANIA TRANSIT CAR NO. 1754: Most of the streetcars at this site are PCC design (Presidents' Conference Committee)—a standardized trolley design originating in the 1930s.

SOUTHERN PENNSYLVANIA TRANSIT CAR NO. 2290: 100 years ago, there were 34,000 miles of trolley tracks. The streetcars, not the automobiles, actually formed the first suburbs.

MBTA PCC TROLLEY INTERIOR: The streetcars are positioned on three rows of track in the woods occupying more than one-third mile.

SEPTA COMMUTER CARS SHARE SPACE WITH THE TROLLEYS: The Septa Car 480 was a Norristown, Pennsylvania, High-Speed Line.

HSTORICAL TROLLEY, PHILADELPHIA, PENNSYLVANIA: Trolleys were in use from the 1800s through the 1960s, but trolley use declined after the Great Depression.

LINE OF BOSTON MBTA CARS: The line of former Boston MBTA streetcars was manufactured between 1945 and 1951 and retired in the early 1990s.

11

WATERSIDE WOOLEN MILL

The industrial revolution spawned the textile industry, and in the early nineteenth century, woolen mills were scattered throughout the eastern part of the United States. I imagine in the days of several eras past, a woolen mill's air was damp and musky with the scent from the sheered sheep fleece.

In the heart of Amish Country, sits a charming woolen mill in Woodbury—The Waterside Woolen Mill ("Mill"). After being idle for more than thirty years, the Mill is fortunate to have some new life flowing within its historical veins. The current owners intend to maintain the authenticity of the mill, weave some natural virgin wool blankets, vests, and other woolen items in the tradition of its former glory while sharing the mill's history with the public.

Established in 1806, the Mill continued operations until the mid-1960s. For a considerable portion of the Mill's operational life, the Yellow Creek of the Meadow Branch River supplied the power for the Mill's operations.

Since 1993, the current owners have been producing traditional woven woolen blankets using the original mill equipment. The mill's antique machinery has been maintained with continuous restoration. The Mill blankets of today are authentic replicas of the material weight, design, weave pattern, and process of those that were used when the operations ceased almost sixty years ago. What is missing within the Mill from a former time? I did not detect a scent of sheered sheep fleece, but I can still imagine this redolence present in the 1800s.

MILL EXTERIOR AND DAM: In the nineteenth century, regional sheep farmers supplied the wool for Waterside Woolen Mill, and the Yellow Creek's water powered the machinery for wool processing.

SPINDLES AND FABRICS: The Mill's antique machinery washed, sorted, picked, oiled, carded, spun, warped, and wove wool blankets.

WARPING AND DRESSING THE LOOM: The yarn is prepared for the loom and involves measuring the yarn and then drawing each thread through the loom.

ASSORTED MILL ANTIQUES: In 1785, William Penn's heirs bequeathed the Mill's land to Abraham Oberholtzer. In 1806, John Snider purchased the property and erected the Mill.

WOOL CARDING MACHINE: Carding cleans, disentangles, and intermixes fibers and produces a continuous mesh for further processing.

ENTRANCE: After being abandoned for approximately thirty years, the grandson of one of the earlier owners purchased the Mill and reintroduced the manufacture of quality woolen blankets and garments according to the Mill's former specifications and processes.

◄ **WOODEN BOBBINS:** In the early days of the Mill, barter played a role in the Mill's daily business. Finished blankets and other woolen products were traded for raw wool and dye.

▼ **WOOL CARDING MACHINE:** While the Mill's ownership saw several owners during the 1800s, it never ceased operations from 1806 until the 1960s.

THIRD FLOOR SPINNING MULE: The spinning mule was used extensively from the late eighteenth century to the early twentieth century for spinning wool into yarn.

SECOND FLOOR LOOM: The Mill has thousands of bobbins. The wool spun into yarn while on the bobbins. The bobbins were then individually loaded onto the looms for the weaving of wool blankets.

12

BEDFORD COUNTY JAIL

The United States is the largest jailer in the world. Jails and prisons are the heart of the United States criminal justice system. According to the United States Bureau of Justice, more than 2 million people are incarcerated in the United States' federal, state, and local prisons and jails.

Although prison systems have changed over time and now reflect modern methods of housing convicted individuals in tandem with rehabilitation, there is, however, a difference between a jail and a prison. Jails are often holding facilities where prisoners await trial or serve a sentence of less than twelve to eighteen months. Prisons hold felons serving sentences of more than one year. The incarcerated person, though, shares a common nightmare across jails and prisons in that simple freedoms are gone, and boredom becomes the daily standard—a barren existence.

For more than 100 years, the Bedford County Jail was in "business." The Bedford County Jail was constructed in 1895 at the cost of $25,000. The Jail is a lovely piece of architecture with its turrets, porches, oak doors, and seven chimneys. Most of the original cells are complete with cots and intact iron bars. At first glance, the Bedford County Jail looks more like a residential mansion than a jail. Abandoned in 2008, the Bedford County Jail is also for sale—jail cells are thrown in as a buyer bonus.

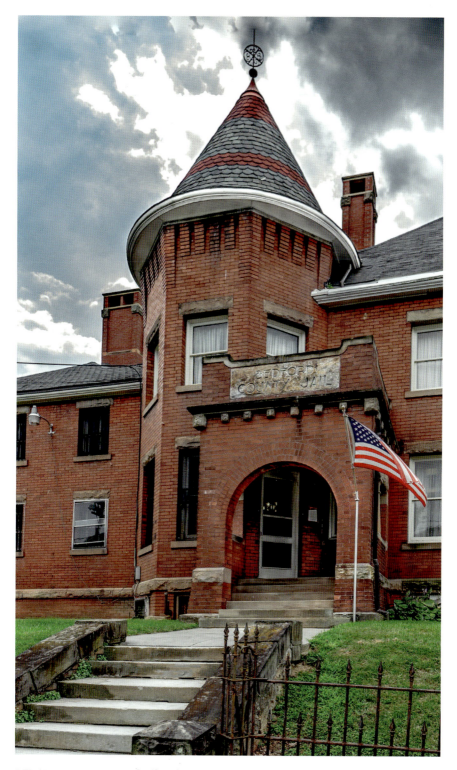

BEDFORD COUNTY JAIL: Bedford County Jail was erected in 1895 by Davis Brothers & Co. of Everett, Pennsylvania. The gothic-inspired jail is for sale, and a hand-weaving studio and craft gallery currently occupies a portion of the jail.

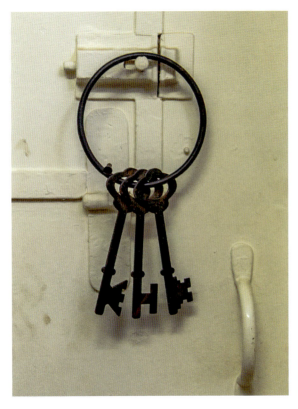

OLD JAIL CELL KEYS: Probation officers lived in the jail until 2008, and after this, Bedford County auctioned the jail.

JAIL CELL: Most of the jail cells still have intact cots and iron bars. The cellblock had one fan directed toward the cellblock hallway.

ONE PHONE CALL: The jail holds a preserved brick oven in the basement. The oven baked the bread for the inmates.

CELL BLOCK WITH INMATE GRAFFITI: The owner of the jail said that a Pittsburgh-area mafia inmate was once confined and hidden in the basement for protection.

13

SCOTLAND SCHOOL FOR VETERANS' CHILDREN

In 1866, two Civil War orphans paved the path for the good fortune of more than ten thousand children. The Scotland School for Veterans' Children ("Scotland School") roots lie with two children begging for food at the Harrisburg governor's mansion pantry door. At this time, Pennsylvania Governor Andrew Curtain spoke to the children and learned of the loss of the orphans' parents during the Civil War. Governor Curtain was dismayed to witness such impoverished offspring of those who had given their lives for the Union. Accordingly, Curtain drove a series of bills in the Pennsylvania General Assembly for the establishment of a statewide network of schools to address the needs of soldiers' orphans.

In 1895, the state-managed Pennsylvania Orphans Industrial School changed to the Scotland School and expanded the primary and secondary education in this private venue to include veterans' children. More than 10,000 students enrolled at the school until its closing in 2009 with many following in their parents' military career footsteps. While operational, the Scotland School provided its pupils with a prime education within a caring setting.

In 2009, state budget constraints forced the closure of the school. The 185-acre campus with seventy structures included a school, gym, pool, theater, library, post office, chapel, trade shops, administration buildings, and housing. Fortunately, the Scotland School has been granted a second chance at life. The Winebrenner Theological Seminary purchased the campus and its buildings in 2013. Upon completion of the Seminary's multi-year restoration plan, an education conference center for a consortium of schools and colleges, theological curriculums, as well as a senior care center will be realized.

SCOTLAND SCHOOL FOR VETERANS' CHILDREN: One of the many buildings on the Scotland School campus.

CLASSROOM: During the Civil War, more than 600,000 lives were lost, with some estimates at 800,000. Many of the Civil War soldiers' orphaned children faced barriers to education, and Scotland School opened to remedy this unfortunate situation.

HALLWAY OF CLASSROOM BUILDING: The land for the Scotland School was purchased for just over $200,000.

HAIR SALON: Carlisle and Boiling Springs competed for the school placement, but Scotland, approximately 4 miles north of Carlisle, won the contract.

POST OFFICE: When enrollment in the Scotland School faded post-Civil War, the school allowed any child of a veteran to attend, and without tuition fees.

THEATER PROJECTION ROOM: In 1951, the state-run school was renamed as the Scotland School for Veterans' Children.

HOME ECONOMICS: Since its opening, the Scotland School for Veterans' Children accepted thousands of students, grades three through twelve, during its 114-year history.

GYMNASIUM: Not only did Scotland students excel in academics, but the Cadets and Red Devils sports teams also realized several sports championships.

NATATORIUM: In 2009, Governor Edward G. Rendell stopped funding for the school, thus forcing its closure.

MUSIC ROOM: Shortly after the school closed, the Winebrenner Theological Seminary purchased the site for $1.8 million.

SHEET MUSIC CLOSET: The Scotland School for Veterans' Children is now known as the Scotland Campus.

SHOOTING RANGE: Before the school closed, many of the children attending the school were underprivileged kids from urban centers.

SHOOTING RANGE TARGETS: In 2009, about 70 percent of the students were Philadelphians.

BOWLING ALLEY: The Scotland Campus is now home to two schools as well as various businesses and organizations.

OFFICE REMAINS: Today's campus offers space for rent for events such as conferences and weddings.

14

COVERED BRIDGE AND GRISTMILL

A covered bridge evokes timeless charm and romance. America has an enduring affection with covered bridges as movies are made about them, books are written about them, and thousands make pilgrimages to covered bridges to contemplate a time when the pace of living was simpler. Covered bridges appeared in the nineteenth century, and were designed for structural support and the provision of shelter during inclement weather, as well as the safe passage of waterway crossings for horses and carriages. Covered bridges love the camera lens and are always photogenic, so after a long day of exploration in Western Pennsylvania, my small group decided to make one more stop on our return to Virginia. We wanted to photograph an abandoned, covered bridge in a thicket of bushes and trees. There is also an abandoned gristmill next to the bridge, but we knew this mill was inaccessible, or so we thought.

Upon arrival at the property that holds the covered bridge, a drove of piglets from the adjacent farm raced toward us for investigation. We spent some time with the curious piglets and then proceeded toward the beautiful bridge for some photographs. A man from the farmhouse near the bridge ambled toward us. This man owned the property that contains the bridge, farm and also the gristmill. The farmer was friendly and warned us not to approach certain cranky adult pigs. He was even more than willing to cite the history of his property. We won the abandoned lottery when my friend charmed the farmer into allowing us a peek inside his gristmill.

The mill was closed for more than eighty years and still holds most of its nineteenth-century milling machinery, as well as a multitude of antique memorabilia and artifacts. We stumbled upon another abandoned time capsule and a mint example of the twilight phase of America's first Industrial Revolution, but well before the commencement of the second Industrial Revolution. It was late afternoon, and the light was vanishing at a rapid rate, so we photographed the fantastic interior contents with haste. I could have spent hours examining the goods within the multi-floored structure.

The mill was constructed in 1852 and closed in 1936 after a devastating flood destroyed the dam supporting the mill. While operational, the mill was powered by water from the nearby creek and produced buckwheat flour, cornmeal, and other feed for livestock.

The lovely Burr Truss design covered bridge dates to 1875, but additional construction in 1892 transformed it into a covered bridge. The 106-foot-long by 13-foot-wide bridge closed in 1982 and remains secluded within its wooded home.

COVERED BRIDGE: The bridge has a medium pitched gable roof and was constructed in 1892. The one span bridge has a Burr Truss design that allows the arch to bear the load of the bridge while the truss keeps the bridge strong and steady.

COVERED BRIDGE: Vintage hand-painted advertisements are still evident on the bridge walls. The bridge is 106 feet long by 13 feet wide.

GRISTMILL REAR: The mill contains a wood lathe and an enclosed water wheel.

GRISTMILL ENTRANCE: The gristmill is a three-story wood frame mill with clapboard siding. The mill contains three sets of millstones, elevators, power gears, and line shafts.

LARGE WOOD SCREW: This device joined with another mechanism to assist the grinding wheel inside the gristmill.

GRISTMILL GEARS: The gears assisted the waterwheel. Waterwheels converted the energy of flowing water for other tasks, such as processing the grain for flour and feed. Waterwheels were widely used before the arrival of electricity in the late nineteenth century.

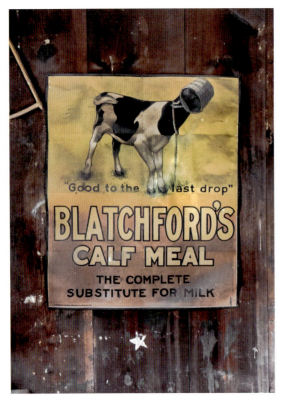

PAPER SIGN ADVERTISEMENT ON GRISTMILL WALL: "Blatchford's Calf Meal, The Original Milk Substitute, Good to the Last Drop"—an early twentieth-century advertisement for milk substitute feed for calves.

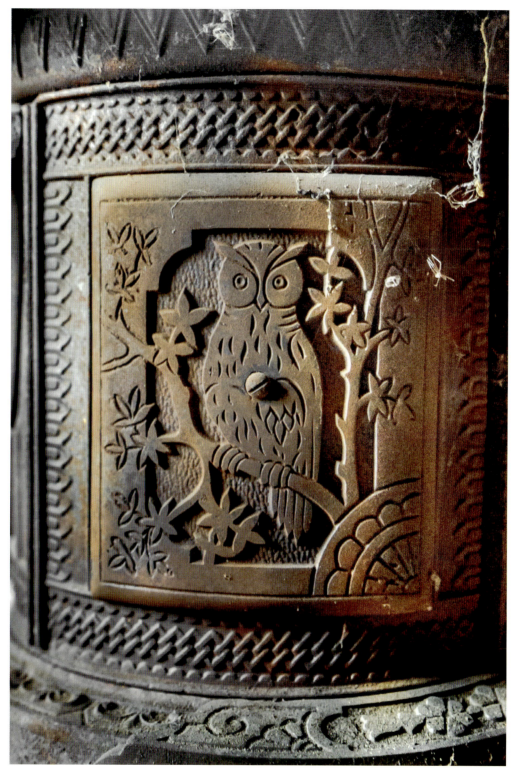

CAST IRON STOVE: Nineteenth-century cast iron stove with ornate owl design on the door is located inside the gristmill.

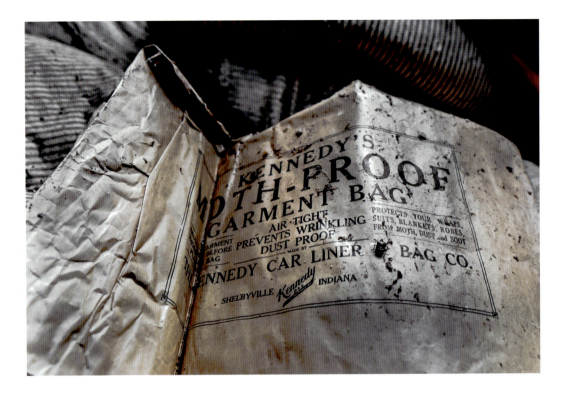

▲ **GARMENT BAGS:** The gristmill had old garment bags for storage and moth prevention of farm clothing. The Kennedy Car Liner Company also produced train car liners for moisture-free grain transport.

◀ **PHOTOGRAPHY INSTRUCTION BOOKS:** Something not normally found inside a nineteenth-to early twentieth-century gristmill—early 1900s instructional photography books. The Kodak Press is the publisher of one of the books.

15
MOOSE LODGE

A Moose Lodge is more than a tavern. Moose Lodge members raise funds and volunteer their time toward community-based needs. The Loyal Order of the Moose, a charitable, fraternal organization, was founded in 1899. In 1898, Dr. John Wilson wanted a fraternal order that was similar to the Elks, but unlike the Masons, and hence, the Moose organization took root. The credo of The Moose is about serving those in need within a local community, especially with assistance to children in unfortunate circumstances.

A visit to an abandoned Moose Lodge in a Western Pennsylvania town was a new urban exploration experience. The lodge was built in 1927 and shut down in 2007 for reasons contrary to the moral guidelines of loyal Moose members.

My exploration group met the current owner of the vacated Moose Lodge who provided the recent colorful history about the establishment. Since Moose membership was waning, perhaps as a result of the regional economic downturn, funds were needed for the maintenance of the Lodge, and generally secured with members' dues. The present owner said the 2007 Lodge's manager became entangled with local illegal drug operations, and once the local police department exposed these transgressions, the Lodge closed at once. The current owner, a proud Vietnam veteran, has plans to transform the site into a military museum.

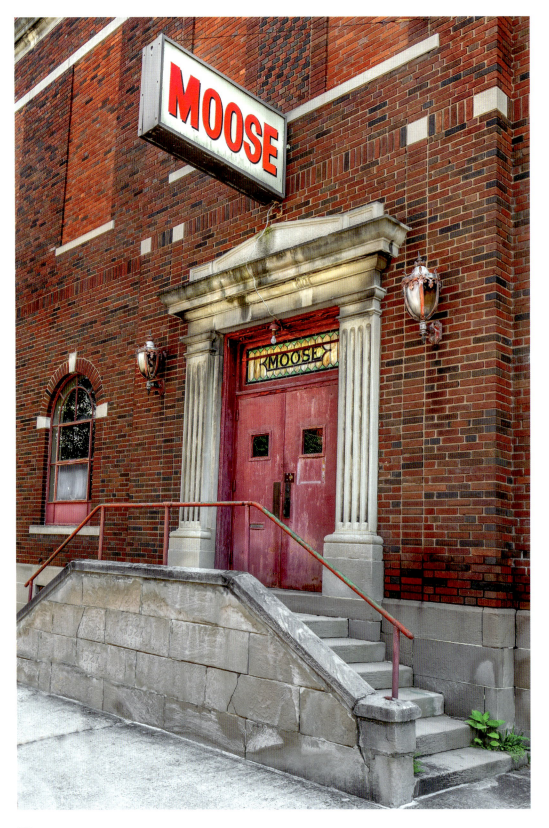

▲ **MOOSE LODGE ARTIFACTS:** Urban explorers often find odd artifacts in abandoned facilities, and this collection of objects, including prosthetic legs, was bereft of logic for contents found inside of a Moose Lodge.

◄ **EXTERIOR OF MOOSE LODGE:** The Loyal Order of Moose organization membership consists of 1 million men in approximately 2,400 lodges in all fifty states, as well as in Canada and Bermuda. The female organization, Women of the Moose, has a 400,000 membership in about 1,600 chapters.

SECOND FLOOR BALLROOM: The second-floor ballroom presents a banner that reads: LOOM (Loyal Order of the Moose) God Bless Mooseheart. The Moose Lodges support the operation of the Chicago based Mooseheart Child City and School serving children in need.

KITCHEN ON SECOND FLOOR/ADJACENT TO BALLROOM: The Chicago based Mooseheart began as a school and expanded into an incorporated community.

CHINA WITH MOOSE LOGO: Four United States Presidents—Warren Harding, Teddy Roosevelt, Franklin D. Roosevelt, and Harry S. Truman—were Moose members.

BAR AND LOUNGE AREA ON FIRST FLOOR: Local Moose units are called Lodges (such as this location), state groups are called State Associations, and the national arm is the Supreme Lodge of the World.

ABOUT THE AUTHOR

CINDY VASKO was born in Allentown, Pennsylvania, and resides in Arlington, Virginia, near Washington D.C. For fifteen years, Cindy was the Publications Manager for a large construction law firm in Northern Virginia, and concurrently, interviewed musicians, wrote articles, and photographed concerts for a music magazine for four years. While Cindy enjoys partaking in all photography genres and is a multi-faceted photographer, she has a passion for abandoned site photography. Cindy is an award-winning photographer, and her works were featured in many gallery exhibitions, including galleries in New York City, Washington D.C., Philadelphia, Pennsylvania, and Paris, France.

BIBLIOGRAPHY

Akron Beacon Journal Staff, "Rust, Grit Mark Pittsburgh's Historic and Colorful Carrie Furnaces That Produced Iron for Steel Making," *Akron Beacon Journal/Ohio*, May 25, 2013, www.ohio.com/akron/lifestyle/rust-grit-mark-pittsburgh-s-historic-and-colorful-carrie-furnaces-that-produced-iron-for-steel-making

Arnold, K., "Preserving Living History At The W. A. Young & Sons Foundry And Machine Shop," *Pennsylvania Historic Preservation*, May 11, 2018, pahistoricpreservation.com/preserving-living-history-young-foundry-machine-shop/

Bellis, M., "The Evolution of the Soda Fountain and the Soft Drink Industry," *ThoughtCo*, September 19, 2017, www.thoughtco.com/history-of-the-soda-fountain-1992432

Bernardini, M., "Scotland School Takes On International Emphasis In New Life," *Public Opinion*, February 10, 2017, www.publicopiniononline.com/story/news/2017/02/10/scotland-school-takes-international-emphasis-new-life/97452586/

Cheney, J., "Hidden History: Inside the Abandoned Cambria Iron Works in Johnstown," *UncoveringPA*, March 17, 2017, uncoveringpa.com/cambria-iron-works-johnstown; "The W.A. Young And Sons Machine Shop And Foundry In Rices Landing, Pennsylvania," *UncoveringPA*, February 24, 2018, uncoveringpa.com/wa-young-and-sons-machine-shop-and-foundry-rices-landing

Christie, L., "7 Fastest Shrinking Cities," *Cable News Network*, April 5, 2013, money.cnn.com/gallery/real_estate/2013/04/05/shrinking-cities/7.html

Collier, S., *et al.*, "The 10 Brands That Built Pittsburgh," *Pittsburgh Magazine*, December 21, 2016, www.pittsburghmagazine.com/Pittsburgh-Magazine/October-2016/The-10-Brands-That-Built-Pittsburgh/index.php?cparticle=9&siarticle=8

Cress, J., "Carlisle Was Possible Location of Orphan School in 1893," *The Sentinel*, July 6, 2018, cumberlink.com/news/local/carlisle-was-possible-location-of-orphan-school-in/article_9d60693b-f31e-56d0-ac75-201eea6644b9.html

Department of the Interior, "National Historic Landmark Nomination W. A. Young & Sons Foundry And Machine Shop Draft," Department of the Interior, 2017, www.nps.gov/orgs/1582/news/LC/fall2016/WAYoungSonsFoundry.pdf

Don, "'Poor' Old Overholt," *Beer & Whiskey Brothers*, October 21, 2009, beerandwhiskeybros.com/2009/10/21/poor-old-overholt/

Duin, J., "Silent Sanctuaries Full of Stories: The Post Gazette Chronicles Pittsburgh's Golden Era," *Get Religion*, December 2, 2016, www.getreligion.org/getreligion/2016/11/28/silent-sanctuaries-full-of-stories-the-post-gazette-chronicles-pittsburghs-golden-era

"Felton's Mill/Felton's Mill & Covered Bridge—Bedford Co.—Pennsylvania," *Mill Pictures*, 2013, www.millpictures.com/mills.php?millid=590&mill=Felten

Fox, R., "A Rust Belt Boom Town Powers Down." *The Huffington Post*, December 31, 2012, www.huffingtonpost.com/randy-fox/mckeesport-pennsylvania-power-house_b_2331973.html

Gehris, J., "On The Whiskey Trail," *Pittsburgh History & Landmarks Foundation*, May 22, 2005, phlf.org/2005/05/22/on-the-whiskey-trail/

Goran, D., "The 1864 Blacksmith Shop—The Most Historically Significant Building Remaining in the Cambria Iron & Steel National Historic Landmark," *The Vintage News*, August 31, 2016, www.thevintagenews.com/2016/06/10/1864-blacksmith-shop-historically-significant-building-remaining-cambria-iron-steel-national-historic-landmark/

Hays, B., "25 Things You Should Know About Pittsburgh," *Mental Floss*, April 7, 2016, mentalfloss.com/article/67611/25-things-you-should-know-about-pittsburgh

Hoover, A., "Why Are Old Green Line Trolleys Wasting Away In Rural Pennsylvania?" *The Boston Globe*, September 6, 2015, www.boston.com/news/untagged/2015/09/06/why-are-old-green-line-trolleys-wasting-away-in-rural-pennsylvania

Hurst, D., and Minemyer, C., "Historic Mill To Be Reborn As Marijuana Growing Site, Officials Say," *The Tribune-Democrat*, August 2, 2018, www.tribdem.com/news/historic-mill-to-be-reborn-as-marijuana-growing-site-officials/article_bd4eb97e-95e6-11e8-8ea7-eb593a4b5763.html

Kennett, L., "Former School To Become Low-Income Elderly Housing," *We Are Central PA*, September 26, 2017, www.wearecentralpa.com/news/former-school-to-become-low-income-elderly-housing/818482302

Komlenic, S., "The True Story Of Old Overholt Rye," *Whisky Advocate*, January 4, 2018, whiskyadvocate.com/true-story-old-overholt-rye/

Library of Congress, "Felten's Mill Covered Bridge, Spanning Brush Creek at Junction of Township Route 386 & State Route 2029, Breezewood, Bedford County, PA," Library of Congress, loc.gov/pictures/item/pa3194/

Logan, R., "Roxbury School To Be Razed This Fall, Making Way For New

Facility," *Daily American*, September 22, 2017, www.dailyamerican.com/ourtownjohnstown/roxbury-school-to-be-razed-this-fall-making-way-for/article_846741e6-9fae-11e7-8d00-bb5dc8bc0bdf.html

Martin, J., "Streetcars: The Transit System America Threw Away," *Governing the States and Localities*, June 2014, www.governing.com/columns/urban-notebook/gov-the-transit-system-we-threw-away.html

Masich, A., *et al.*, "The Way We Were," *Pittsburgh Magazine*, December 2013, www.pittsburghmagazine.com/Pittsburgh-Magazine/December-2013/The-Way-We-Were/

Maurer, P. I., "Abandoned States: Pennsylvania's Streetcar Graveyard," *DCist,* July 15, 2016, dcist.com/2015/07/abandoned_states_the_streetcar_grav.php

McKinsey, F., *et al.*, "History of Frederick County, Maryland in Two Volumes. Volume I," *Clearfield* , 2012

Mihm, S., "How The U.S. Squandered Its Steel Superiority," *Bloomberg*, March 5, 2018, www.bloomberg.com/view/articles/2018-03-05/steel-history-shows-how-america-lost-ground-to-europe

Miller, M., "The Waterside Woolen Mill," *Only in the Cove*, November 8, 2014, www.onlyinthecove.com/the-waterside-woolen-mill/

New Castle News Staff, "Society To Hear History Of Shenango China," *New Castle News*, May 3, 2012, www.ncnewsonline.com/news/local_news/society-to-hear-history-of-shenango-china/article_a722ade2-f72e-5f36-9fa0-f083316713f8.html

Niedbala, B., "W. A. Young & Sons Foundry In Rices Landing Designated A National Landmark," *Observer-Reporter*, January 16, 2017, observer-reporter.com/news/localnews/w-a-young-sons-foundry-in-rices-landing-designated-a/article_b8e9339e-0592-55fd-b4b2-d7ec154c59eb.html

Niederberger, M., "Locking The Doors: Tears And Memories Mark Parishioners' Farewell To 103-Year-Old St. Stephen Hungarian Church," *Post Gazette*, July 10, 2002, old.post-gazette.com/neigh_south/20020710sstephen0710p2.asp

Oneill, T., "Elks, Shriners, And Masons: How 'Old Man' Frats Got Their Names And Symbols," *This Week*, February 21, 2014, theweek.com/articles/450722/elks-shriners-masons-how-old-man-frats-got-names-symbols

Origjanska, M., "Windber Trolley Graveyard: An Apocalyptic Trolley Graveyard Sitting Deep In The Woods Of Pennsylvania," *The Vintage News*, February 27, 2018, www.thevintagenews.com/2018/02/27/windber-trolley-graveyard-2/

Papa, R., "Cambria Iron Works," *Carnegie Melon University*, 2008, www.cmu.edu/steinbrenner/brownfields/Case%20Studies/pdf/cambria%20iron%20works%20case%20study.pdf

"Pittsburgh: St. Stephen Roman Catholic," *Peeling Walls Blog*, June 23, 2016, peelingwalls.com/2016/06/23/pittsburgh-st-stephen-roman-catholic/

Richards, D., "Johnstown Plans To Demolish 25 Abandoned Homes, But Hundreds More Remain," *WJAC*, August 9, 2018, wjactv.com/news/local/johnstown-plans-to-demolish-25-abandoned-homes-but-hundreds-more-remain

Ryan, D. B., "History of Shenango China," *USA Today/Gannett Satellite Information Network*, April 17, 2017, traveltips.usatoday.com/history-shenango-china-21506.html

Saint Stephen (McKeesport), Catholic Diocese of Pittsburgh, 2018, diopitt.org/saint-stephen-mckeesport

"Steel Footprints," *Rivers of Steel*, 2018, www.riversofsteel.com/map/category/503/P360/

Stromberg, J., "The Real Story Behind The Demise Of America's Once-Mighty Streetcars," *Vox*, May 7, 2015, www.vox.com/2015/5/7/8562007/streetcar-history-demise

Van Horn, B. F., "Bible, Axe, And Plow," *Northern Bedford County School District*, 1986, www.nbcsd.org/cms/lib/PA01001217/Centricity/Domain/5/BibleAxePlow.pdf

Vincent, S., "Flipping the Plate: Changing Perceptions of the Shenango China Company, 1945–1991," *Kent University*, 2010

Whitaker, H., "Top Ten Things To Remember When Closing A Church," *Episcopal Cafe*, August 7, 2016, www.episcopalcafe.com/top-ten-things-to-remember-when-closing-a-church/

Wondrich, D., "How Pennsylvania Rye Whiskey Lost Its Way," *The Daily Beast*, September 12, 2016, www.thedailybeast.com/how-pennsylvania-rye-whiskey-lost-its-way?ref=scroll